To:

From:

Dogs
Are Special

GRAMERCY BOOKS
NEW YORK

Published by Gramercy Books, an imprint of Random House Value Publishing, a division of Random House, Inc., New York.

Gramercy is a registered trademark and the colophon is a trademark of Random House, Inc.

Random House
New York • Toronto • London • Sydney • Auckland
www.randomhouse.com

Compiled by Kira Baum
Interior design by Christine Kell

Printed and bound in China

Library of Congress Cataloging-in-Publication Data

Dogs are special : a tribute to our noble companions.
    p. cm.
  ISBN: 978-0-517-22883-8
    1. Dogs–Quotations, maxims, etc. 2. Dogs–Pictorial works.

PN6084.D64.D66 2007
636.7—dc22

                                                    2006043545

10 9 8 7 6 5 4 3 2 1

Acknowledgments: 1, *Brand X Pictures/Jupiter Images.* 3, *Corbis.* 5, *Corbis.* 7, *PhotoAlto/SuperStock.* 9, *BananaStock/Jupiter Images.* 11, *Corbis.* 12-13, *PhotoAlto/SuperStock.* 14, *Photodisc/Punchstock.* 17, *PhotoAlto/SuperStock.* 19, *Brand X Pictures/ Jupiter Images.* 21, *Corbis.* 22, *Corbis.* 24-25, *Brand X Pictures/SuperStock.* 27, *Image Source Ltd./age fotostock.* 29, *Image Source/Punchstock.* 31, *Stan Fellerman/Alamy.* 32-33, *Juniors Bildarchiv/Alamy.* 34, *Corbis.* 37, *Brand X Pictures/Jupiter Images.* 39, *Pixtal/SuperStock.* 40-41, *image100/SuperStock.* 43, *Pixtal/age fotostock.* 44, *Digital Vision.* 47, *Image Source Ltd./age fotostock.* 49, *Juniors Bildarchiv/Alamy.* 50-51, *Corbis.* 53, *Pixtal/age fotostock.* 55, *Corbis.* 56, *imagebroker/Alamy.* 58-59, *Designpics.com/Punchstock.* 61, *Pixtal/age fotostock.* 63, *Pixtal/age fotostock.* 64, *Image Source Ltd./age fotostock.*

Dogs
Are Special

Happiness is a warm puppy.

CHARLES M. SCHULZ

There is no psychiatrist in the world like a puppy licking your face.

BERNARD WILLIAMS

My goal in life is to become as wonderful as my dog thinks I am.

UNKNOWN

The greatest love is a mother's; then comes a dog's;
then comes a sweetheart's.

POLISH PROVERB

He is your friend, your partner, your defender, your dog.
You are his life, his love, his leader. He will be yours, faithful
and true, to the last beat of his heart. You owe it to him to
be worthy of such devotion.

UNKNOWN

Mark what a generosity and courage [a dog] will
put on when he finds himself maintained by a man,
who to him is instead of a God.

FRANCIS BACON

The better I get to know men, the more I find myself loving dogs.

CHARLES DE GAULLE

It's funny how dogs and cats know the inside
of folks better than other folks do, isn't it?

ELEANOR H. PORTER, *Pollyanna*

Love me, love my dog.

LATIN SAYING

A dog is man's best friend.

SAYING

Our culture makes severe demands on the dog. We humans accept, mostly on hearsay, the premise that "dog is man's best friend" and let it go at that. For the dog, this is a debatable issue. He knows that, if anything, the reverse holds true. It is man who is dog's best friend.

STEPHEN BAKER, *How to Live With a Neurotic Dog*

Like master, like dog.

SAYING

The dog...commends himself to our favor by affording play to our propensity for mastery.

THORSTEIN VEBLEN

We are alone, absolutely alone on this chance planet: and, amid all the forms of life that surround us, not one, excepting the dog, has made an alliance with us.

MAURICE MAETERLINCK

If man was what he ought to be, he would be adored by the animals.

HENRI AMIEL

Owners may have difficulty understanding their dogs. On the other hand, dogs have no trouble at all understanding their owners.

STEPHEN BAKER, *Games Dogs Play*

Dogs are better than human beings because they know but do not tell.

EMILY DICKINSON

The more I see of men the more I like dogs.

MADAME DE STAEL

If you have men who will exclude any of God's creatures from the shelter of compassion and pity, you will have men who will deal likewise with their fellow men.

ST. FRANCIS OF ASSISI

Like all dogs, Skip was colorblind. He made friends easily with people of all races and origins. The town was segregated back then, but as we know, dogs are a whole lot smarter than people.

WILLIE MORRIS, *My Dog Skip*

I am I because my little dog knows me but, creatively speaking the little dog knowing that you are you and your recognising that he knows, that is what destroys creation. That is what makes school.

GERTRUDE STEIN

I started Early—Took my Dog—
And visited the Sea—

EMILY DICKINSON

My little dog—a heartbeat at my feet.

EDITH WHARTON

16

In order to really enjoy a dog, one doesn't merely try to train him to be semihuman. The point of it is to open oneself to the possibility of becoming partly a dog.

EDWARD HOAGLAND, "Dogs and the Tug of Life"

The great pleasure of a dog is that you may make a fool of yourself with him and not only will he not scold you, but he will make a fool of himself too.

SAMUEL BUTLER

If you pick up a starving dog and make him prosperous, he will not bite you. This is the principal difference between a dog and a man.

MARK TWAIN

I love a dog. He does nothing for political reasons.

Will Rogers

These Republican leaders have not been content with attacks on me, or my wife, or on my sons. No, not content with that, they now include my little dog Fala. Well, of course I don't resent attacks, but Fala does resent them. You know, Fala is Scotch, and being a Scottie, learning that the Republican fiction writers in Congress and out had concocted a story that I had left him behind on the Aleutian Islands and had sent a destroyer back to find him—at a cost to the tax payers of two or three, or eight or twenty million dollars—his Scotch soul was furious. He has not been the same dog since.

Franklin D. Roosevelt

If you want a friend in Washington, get a dog.

Harry S. Truman

FROM "OLD DOG TRAY"

Old dog Tray's ever faithful;
  Grief can not drive him away;
He is gentle, he is kind—
  I shall never, never find
A better friend than old dog Tray!

STEPHEN COLLINS FOSTER

The Gift which I am sending you is called a dog, and is in fact
the most precious and valuable possession of mankind.

THEODORUS GAZA,
"Laudation Canis: An Address to Mohammed II"

Heaven goes by favor; if it went by merit, you would
stay out and your dog would go in.

MARK TWAIN

Dogs are not our whole life, but they make our lives whole.

ROGER CARAS

When a dog runs at you, whistle for him.

HENRY DAVID THOREAU

No matter how little money and how few possessions you own,
having a dog makes you rich.

LOUIS SABIN

I care not for a man's religion whose dog and cat are not the better for it.

ABRAHAM LINCOLN

You can say any foolish thing to a dog, and the
dog will give you a look that says, 'My God, you're right!
I never would've thought of that!'

DAVE BARRY

A bond with a true dog is as lasting as
the ties of this earth will ever be.

KONRAD LORENZ

I used to look at (my dog) Smokey and think, "If you were a little
smarter you could tell me what you were thinking," and he'd look at me
like he was saying, "If you were a little smarter, I wouldn't have to."

FRED JUNGCLAUS

I love dogs. They live in the moment and don't care about
anything except affection and food. They're loyal and happy.
Humans are just too damn complicated.

DAVID DUCHOVNY

Acquiring a dog may be the only opportunity
a human ever has to choose a relative.

MORDECAI WYATT JOHNSON

One day Dad says to Mum, "Either I go, or
some of these bloody dogs have to go."
"But they don't have anywhere *to* go."
Dad is in a rage. He aims a kick at a cluster of
dogs, who cheerfully return his gesture with
jump-up licking let's-playfulness.
Mum says, "See? How sweet."

ALEXANDRA FULLER,
Don't Let's Go to the Dogs Tonight

The world was conquered through the understanding of dogs;
the world exists through the understanding of dogs.

FRIEDRICH NIETZSCHE

Money will buy you a fine dog,
but only love can make it wag its tail.

RICHARD FRIEDMAN

But a dog teaches a boy fidelity, perseverance, and to turn around three times before lying down—very important traits in times like these. In fact, just as soon as a dog comes along who, in addition to these qualities, also knows when to buy and sell stocks, he can be moved right up to the boy's bedroom and the boy can sleep in the dog house.

ROBERT BENCHLEY, *Chips Off the Old Benchley*

Yesterday I was a dog. Today I'm a dog. Tomorrow I'll probably still be a dog. Sigh! There's so little hope for advancement.

CHARLES M. SCHULZ

Did you ever walk into a room and forget why you walked in?
I think that's how dogs spend their lives.

SUE MURPHY

Living with a dog is messy—like living with an idealist.

H. L. MENCKEN

Dogs feel very strongly that they should always go with you
in the car, in case the need should arise for them to bark
violently at nothing right in your ear.

DAVE BARRY

Some puppies begin their study of humans at the pet shop as they watch
the crowd gather outside the window. Pretending to be hard at play, they
can observe their future owners make fools of themselves in every way.
They wiggle their eyebrows up and down, stick out their tongues, smack
their lips, tap dance, blow kisses, froth at the mouth, snap their fingers,
clap their hands, press their noses against the glass and otherwise try to
prove that underneath it all they have a sense of humor.

STEPHEN BAKER, *Games Dogs Play*

The most affectionate creature in the world is a wet dog.

AMBROSE BIERCE

If you think dogs can't count, try putting three dog biscuits in your
pocket and then giving Fido only two of them.

PHIL PASTORET

Dachshund: A half-a-dog high and a dog-and-a-half long.

HENRY LOUIS MENCKEN

I poured spot remover on my dog. Now he's gone.

STEPHEN WRIGHT

If you are a dog and your owner suggests that you wear a sweater ...
suggest that he wear a tail.

FRAN LEBOWITZ, "Pointers for Pets"

The dog is a yes-animal. Very popular with
people who can't afford a yes man.

ROBERTSON DAVIES

AAH! You ate my homework?...
I didn't know dogs really did that.

BART SIMPSON, "The Simpsons"

My husband and I are either going to buy a dog or have a child.
We can't decide whether to ruin our carpet or ruin our lives.

RITA RUDNER

"I'm afraid of dogs," he said. "I've had some pretty bad experiences
with them." I told this to Grandfather, who was still half of himself
in dream. "No one is afraid of dogs," he said. "Grandfather informs
me that no one is afraid of dogs."

JONATHAN SAFRAN FOER, *Everything Is Illuminated*

I hope if dogs take over the world, and they choose a king,
they don't just go by size, because I bet there are some
Chihuahuas with some good ideas.

JACK HANDY

A dog will make eye contact. A cat will, too, but a cat's eyes don't even look entirely warm-blooded to me, whereas a dog's eyes look human except less guarded. A dog will look at you as if to say, "What do you want me to do for you? I'll do anything for you." Whether a dog can in fact, do anything for you if you don't have sheep (I never have) is another matter. The dog is willing.

ROY BLOUNT JR. *"Dogs Vis-à-vis Cats," Now Where Were We?*

In order to keep a true perspective of one's importance, everyone should have a dog that will worship him and a cat that will ignore him.

UNKNOWN

The dog is mentioned in the Bible eighteen times— the cat not even once.

W. E. FARBSTEIN

Cats are the ultimate narcissists. You can tell this because of all the time they spend on personal grooming. Dogs aren't like this. A dog's idea of personal grooming is to roll in a dead fish. Dogs spend their time thinking about doing good deeds for their masters, or sleeping.

JAMES GORMAN

You call to a dog and a dog will break its neck to get to you. Dogs just want to please. Call to a cat and its attitude is, "What's in it for me?"

LEWIS GRIZZARD

When one dog barks at a shadow, a hundred bark at the sound.

CHINESE PROVERB

I wonder if other dogs think poodles are members of a weird religious cult.

RITA RUDNER

The meeting in the open of two dogs, strangers to each other, is one of the most painful, thrilling, and pregnant of all conceivable encounters; it is surrounded by an atmosphere of the last canniness, presided over by a constraint for which I have no preciser name; they simply cannot pass each other, their mutual embarrassment is frightful to behold.

THOMAS MANN

Dogs have so many friends because they wag
their tails, not their tongues.

UNKNOWN

A dog wags its tail with its heart.

MARTIN BUXBAUM

My favorite story is about the monk who said to a Master,
"Has a dog Buddha-nature too?" The Master replied, "Wu"—which
is what the dog himself would have said.

GILBERT HIGHET

A dog has the soul of a philosopher.

PLATO

Dog: A kind of additional or subsidiary Deity designed to
catch the overflow and surplus of the world's worship.

AMBROSE BIERCE

All knowledge, the totality of all questions and all
answers is contained in the dog.

FRANZ KAFKA

That they may have a little peace, even the best dogs are
compelled to snarl occasionally.

WILLIAM FEATHER

It's not the size of the dog in the fight,
it's the size of the fight in the dog.

MARK TWAIN

52

If you don't own a dog, at least one, there is not necessarily anything
wrong with you, but there may be something wrong with your life.

ROGER CARAS

No one appreciates the very special genius of
your conversation as the dog does.

CHRISTOPHER MORLEY

The only creatures that are evolved enough to convey
pure love are dogs and infants.

JOHNNY DEPP

Dogs love their friends and bite their enemies,
quite unlike people, who are incapable of
pure love and always have to mix love and
hate in their object-relations.

SIGMUND FREUD

God…sat down for a moment when the dog was finished in order to
watch it…and to know that it was good, that nothing was lacking,
that it could not have been made better.

RAINER MARIA RILKE

All dogs go to heaven because, unlike people,
dogs are naturally good and loyal and kind.

All Dogs Go to Heaven

The dog is a gentleman; I hope to go to his heaven, not man's.

MARK TWAIN

God will prepare everything for our perfect happiness in heaven,
and if it takes my dog being there, I believe he'll be there.

BILLY GRAHAM

Life is a series of dogs.

GEORGE CARLIN

You think dogs will not be in heaven?
I tell you, they will be there long before any of us.

ROBERT LOUIS STEVENSON

I came across a photograph of him not long ago, his black face
with the long snout sniffing at something in the air, his tail straight
and pointing, his eyes flashing in some momentary excitement.
Looking at a faded photograph taken more than forty years before,
even as a grown man, I would admit I still missed him.

WILLIE MORRIS, "My Dog Skip"

She was growing old now and so was Flush. She bent down over
him for a moment. Her face with its wide mouth and its great
eyes and its heavy curls was still oddly like his. Broken asunder,
yet made in the same mould, each, perhaps, completed what was
dormant in the other. But she was woman; he was dog.

VIRGINIA WOOLF, *Flush: A Biography*

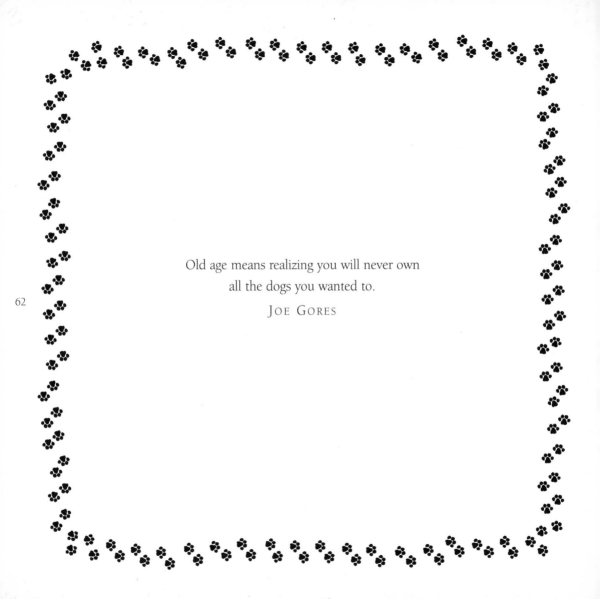

Old age means realizing you will never own
all the dogs you wanted to.

JOE GORES